D0172890

Toilet Train Your Cat,
Plain and Simple

Toilet Train Your Cat,
Plain and Simple

An Incredible, Practical, Foolproof
Guide to #1 and #2

Clifford Brooks

Illustrations by Stephanie Medeiros

Skyhorse Publishing

Copyright © 2017 by Clifford Brooks

All rights reserved. No part of this book may be reproduced in any manner without the express written consent of the publisher, except in the case of brief excerpts in critical reviews or articles. All inquiries should be addressed to Skyhorse Publishing, 307 West 36th Street, 11th Floor, New York, NY 10018.

Skyhorse Publishing books may be purchased in bulk at special discounts for sales promotion, corporate gifts, fund-raising, or educational purposes. Special editions can also be created to specifications. For details, contact the Special Sales Department, Skyhorse Publishing, 307 West 36th Street, 11th Floor, New York, NY 10018 or info@skyhorsepublishing.com.

Skyhorse® and Skyhorse Publishing® are registered trademarks of Skyhorse Publishing, Inc.®, a Delaware corporation.

Visit our website at www.skyhorsepublishing.com.

10 9 8 7 6 5 4 3 2 1

Library of Congress Cataloging-in-Publication Data is available on file.

Cover design by Jane Sheppard
Cover illustration by Stephanie Medeiros
Interior illustrations by Stephanie Medeiros

Print ISBN: 978-1-5107-0725-2
eBook ISBN: 978-1-5107-0726-9

Printed in China

Dedication

This book is dedicated to my big sister, Ruth Woods, for her support, her patience, and her unconditional love. But most importantly, for teaching what it means to be family.

Table of Contents

Why Toilet Train Your Cat?

Imagine waking up in the morning, your cat nuzzling your cheek, eager for his morning meal. You nuzzle back and the clean smell of feline fur fills your nose. Even though his morning duties are done, there's no telltale litter box odor to contend with.

You get up and pad across the floor to the bathroom. For the first time in memory there's no gravelly crunch under your bare feet, no scattered litter to sweep up, and no smelly box to sift through. All you have to do is flush.

Sound like a fantasy? It doesn't have to be. In a few short months, you could be living a litter-free existence. If you've ever considered training your cat to use the toilet but haven't done anything about it, now is the time.

Did I say a few months? The reality is that training a cat to use the toilet takes time and patience. It's a step-by-step process that capitalizes on your cat's natural abilities and inclinations. I've heard of people training their cats in a couple of weeks but those cats are the rare exception to the rule. So plan on three solid months, give or take a week or two, to completely toilet train your cat. I've found that, no matter how smart or stubborn a cat may be, in approximately three months you will say good-bye to litter and litter boxes forever.

If it still sounds rather daunting, trust me as I lead you through the process. The first time your cat nonchalantly hops up on the toilet and does his business, you'll realize it was well worth the effort.

Real Expectations

A toilet-trained cat has few, if any, drawbacks. Your cat, already a fastidiously clean animal, will become even more so. Because he[1] will no longer come in contact with his waste, his fur will stay clean and odor free. As an additional benefit, you'll no longer have to worry about the ill effects of commercial cat litter on the environment or your cat.

You will have to remember to flush for him. Though not unheard of, your cat is not likely to learn to flush. That said, your cat will want to do something about the odor. My cats pulled the toilet paper from the roll and stuffed it in the toilet. It wouldn't have been a bad solution if I could have taught them some restraint—they used about half a roll each time! After putting the toilet paper out of reach, one of my cats would push the door and run out before it closed, trapping the odor inside. Both of these solutions illustrate the intelligence and resourcefulness of the cat. During the training process, you will need to respond promptly to your cat's actions so he doesn't get put off and decide that the toilet is an unsuitable alternative. Moving the toilet paper and purchasing a motion-activated air freshener[2] made my cats very happy. You will be amazed at how clever and resourceful your cat is as you guide him through the process.

My cats have been using the toilet happily for years, so every once in a while I put the toilet paper back on the roll. All is well for a while, and then one day, seemingly out of the blue, I walk in to find a bowl full of paper. I smile, clean up, remove the roll,

---

1   For simplicity, I've chosen to refer to your cat as male, and though I use the singular, the process is applicable to those training multiple cats.
2   Don't use an automatic air freshener until after you have fully trained your cat. Stick with a solid or spray during the training period so as not to startle your cat.

and place it on the back of the toilet. I decided a long time ago that a displaced toilet paper roll was a small price to pay for the savings, convenience, and joy of sharing my home with a pair of toilet-trained cats.

Learning a New Behavior

Cats are extremely trainable, but in my experience, they learn "tricks" when the trick fills a particular need or the reward is pretty much irresistible. For the most part, they don't learn tricks to please you. Without self-motivation, they see no reason for the trick and are not swayed by earthly coercion, no matter how earnest. It doesn't mean your cat doesn't love you—it just doesn't feel the need to perform in order to earn your love and admiration. Many cats tend to have a "love me as I am" attitude, and if you do, they return it tenfold.

Fortunately, teaching a cat to use the toilet is nothing like teaching him a silly parlor trick. You will be providing your cat with an alternative to a litter box or a soft patch of ground. So forget about tricks—that's not what this is all about. You will be teaching your cat a series of small changes that add up to a really big deal.

Make no mistake though, the transition isn't without its stresses. Unfortunately, you can't tell your cat why you're imposing all these little changes—often daily changes—on his routine, so don't expect him to take it silently. Expect a little meowing, especially during the latter stages of training, as your cat recovers from his litter dependency and replaces it with a series of new behaviors.

As you go through the process, it may help to remember the last time your routine got changed and how, despite knowing the reason for the change, you struggled with it. Allow your cat to complain a little and act out as he grudgingly adopts a whole new set of behaviors which, one day, will come to him as naturally as the old ones.

You will also have to deal with a bit of a mess as your cat may kick a lot of the dwindling litter store about as he gets used to the new setup. Once your cat has accepted the toilet, things should be nice and relatively tidy, but until then, expect a little more litter strewn around than normal. You'll also have to deal with walking into the bathroom to face a bowl full of cat excrement and the lingering odor of a toilet that hasn't been flushed. Flush the toilet, spray a little air freshener if necessary, and move on to other tasks.

And finally, there's the issue of accidents. During the training process, you will have to deal with your cat going in inappropriate places a few times. It will happen, but once your cat decides that the toilet is a great place to do his business, you shouldn't have to worry about accidents anymore.

Why Me?

I'm not an animal behaviorist, a veterinarian, or a zoologist. I'm just a guy who decided that living with a toilet-trained cat would be awesome. So I made it my mission to do so. But where to begin? The few products and resources I encountered were lacking in one way or another, and one particular product, sold in pet shops across the country, failed miserably. There are better options out there today (I trained my first cat over twenty years ago), and because of a proliferation of clever cats in the media and on YouTube, more and more people are realizing that toilet training a cat is not only desirable but possible. I wrote this guide with those people in mind.

And let's be honest. If you're reading this, you probably think there's something adorable about watching your cat jump up on the toilet and using it like a human. All these years later, I still get a kick out of it.

The process is a bit daunting and even a bit scary as you see your perfectly litter box–trained cat struggling with something new. Is my method better than the others? Foolproof? I don't know, but I wouldn't be sharing this if I didn't think my method was the most straightforward and cost-effective solution out there. Over the years, I've personally trained seven cats to use the toilet: three domestic cats, two F1 hybrids, an F2 hybrid, and a wild yet wonderful Bengal. All were champs, all had their own particular needs and quirks, and all took relatively the same amount of time to fully train. The disparate collection of cats I've trained has me feeling pretty confident that my method will work on even the most stubborn and intractable cat out there. That said, it will require patience and perseverance on your part. If you get frustrated and give up easily, toilet training your cat might not be for you and may result in a miserable experience for both you and your cat. Be honest with yourself: do you have the patience necessary to shepherd your cat through the process?

As a lifelong apartment dweller, I can't tell you how wonderful it has been to not have to drag home jugs of litter, find a suitable location for a box when none exists, and worry about the nonstop cleaning. But even more important than the lifestyle change it's afforded, I learned, during the process, a lot about my cats and how, by exhibiting care and understanding, the sky is the limit.

Okay, let's get started!

Guaranteed Success?

While there are no guarantees in life, if you're tenacious, creative, consistent, and caring, I see no reason why you won't be just as successful as I've been. I've included as much information as possible—reaching back in my memory to the time when I trained my first cat—to address the questions and concerns you may have.

As long as your cat is healthy and consistently using the litter box, you should be able to get him to use the toilet instead.

Important Note: If your cat is not using the litter box regularly, you will need to deal with that issue first. Take your cat to the vet and get a clean medical bill of health, and then identify any environmental or social issues that may be causing his lapses. Until you've resolved this issue and your cat is regularly using the litter box, don't attempt to begin the process.

Encouragement versus Training

Semantics? No, not really. When teaching your cat to use the toilet, you'll be encouraging him to adopt a new series of behaviors. In a real sense, your cat knows how to use the toilet, he just sees no reason to do so. Having trained a half dozen cats to use the toilet, I'm convinced of it. Knowledge, in this case, is definitely power. Don't force. Encourage. Provide the impetus for your cat to agree to the desired behavioral changes, and you'll be on your way.

Lessons Learned

It's easy to become impatient while working through the steps, and at times, it will seem like you aren't making any progress. But you are. At the end of each step, the **Lessons Learned** section identifies the behaviors your cat has just picked up.

Progress Journal

In the back of the book is a Progress Journal that you can use to track your cat's progress. There is a page for each step where you can post a picture of your setup or your cat, add notes on how the training is going, and log the start date and completion date for each step.

The Progress Journal is your place to jot down the funny, the problematic, and the little successes along the way. When you complete the process, you'll have a record that you can share and even utilize during future trainings.

While journaling the process is optional, it's highly recommended. Some of the benefits of using the journal include:

- Months or years from now, looking back over the journal will remind you of the difficult yet rewarding process your cat went through. Once he's using the toilet regularly, it's easy to forget how proud you were the first time he got it right.

- It serves as a place to identify issues as you work through the steps. If things seem to take a turn for the worse, you may need to back up a step or two. Your notes will help you identify where and when things went south.

- You can't help but make some observations about your cat's nature. Write them down as they can enhance your relationship with your cat.

- Keep track of successful task completion. For instance, your cat may need to successfully complete the desired task 3–4 times before moving on—this provides a place to tally his successes.

- Write down reminders for yourself.

- Share your notebook with friends and family who also want to toilet train their cats. While buying them a copy of this book will serve as the basis of their training, being able to read about your successes and failures will add a personal touch and encourage them to carry on.

- On bad days, reading back over the progress your cat has made, the hurdles you've jumped together, will provide confidence that the current problem will pass, too.

- On those days where everything seems to be going awry, sit down, take a breath, and write down what's going on. Trust me, by the time you've written it down, your blood pressure will go down, you'll see the situation for what it really is, and you'll be able to move forward.

Journaling can mean the difference between failure and success for some. The little successes are often hard to see; writing them down and going over them from time to time can make them more real in your mind and make you proud of your cat's progress.

As you should be.

So, sharpen your pencil and your observational skills. It won't take much time and will be well worth the effort.

Before You Begin

B efore you begin the process, there are a few things that must be assembled:

- 10-quart plastic mixing/food storage bowl
- Flushable litter
- Cat rewards
- Pet stain remover/odor neutralizer
- A couple plastic rulers (optional)
- Old magazines, boxes, paper

That's it. Not much, really, when you consider how much you're bound to save in the years ahead. And if you consider the fact that you have to buy litter anyway, the price is even lower. As an apartment dweller, I used to buy litter, litter box deodorizers, and little plastic bags to scoop the dirty litter into. It added up pretty quickly. Now I walk past the litter in the pet store with barely a sideways glance. That, my friends, is living!

The materials are few, but they are important and deserve a closer look.

Plastic mixing/food storage bowl: You will need a plastic bowl to insert into the toilet. You may already have one of these in the

cupboard and won't have to buy one (of course, if it's not yours, ask first; you won't be using it to serve popcorn ever again). My first bowl was a repurposed white plastic mixing bowl. Because the bowl was a little small, I taped a ruler to the lip on both sides of the bowl to securely "hang" it in the toilet. Once the seat was lowered, the bowl was secure enough for my 18-pound cat to use confidently.

On the other hand, rather than using the ruler method, you'd be better off purchasing an inexpensive flexible plastic bowl that has a little bit of a lip along the edge. A plastic 10-quart mixing bowl is likely to fit right in, with the lip of the mixing bowl clamped between the seat and the bowl, creating a secure seal.

I've got one of those generic white porcelain toilets, but I'm aware that some people have decorator colors. If you have one of the more colorful bowls, try to find a mixing bowl of the same color. For some, that might be difficult, but it should make the eventual removal of the bowl less noticeable and jarring. Anything you can do to make your cat less anxious during the process will make things easier for you both.

Litter: Make sure that the litter you choose is a flushable variety. I've seen flushable litter made from corn cob, pine, wheat, and clay. Try finding a litter that closely approximates the litter your cat has become accustomed to. If you've been using a clumping clay litter all along, it would be best to search for a clay-based flushable litter. If your cat is particularly resistant to change, get your cat used to the new litter by switching to it before beginning the process.

Cat rewards: Many cats respond favorably to commercial cat treats. They're easy to store and use, so if your cat enjoys commercially prepared treats, they make an ideal training reward. On the other hand, if your cat prefers a chunk of cheese, make that his reward. One of my cats, a particularly stodgy and stubborn tom, turned his nose up at treats offered as rewards. He didn't want to have any part of this new-fangled potty thing, so the offering of a treat as he stepped down from the bowl added insult to injury. For him, I was able to reward him by brushing the side of his face with his favorite brush—something he couldn't resist. So, from here on out, when I refer to rewards, I'm not just talking about food treats, but whatever it is that makes your cat purr.

Again, be creative. Find something your cat craves and relegate it to his post-performance reward. That means, as harsh as it sounds, no between-performance rewards. Okay, fewer between-performance rewards.

In addition to the rewards, don't forget the accolades! Always tell your cat what a wonderful guy he is, stroking him affectionately all the while. Even if your cat appears unappreciative and shies away, don't despair. It's getting through to him. Trust me on this one, and soon you may have a cat that finds the post-performance accolades the real reward.

As you progress through the program and your cat begins to use the toilet consistently, reduce the number of rewards. If you don't, you might end up with a cat who waits to eliminate until you get home.

Pet stain remover/odor neutralizer: If you're going to skimp on anything, make sure it's not here. Cat urine is very difficult to completely eradicate. Most household cleaners just aren't adequate and some, especially those that contain ammonia, may even attract the cat, enticing him to void himself in the same spot again. Products designed specifically to neutralize pet stains and odors are available at your local pet store. But don't wait until your cat has made his first mistake. You'll want to have it on hand when that mistake occurs. Trust me, even if your cat has never even considered going in an inappropriate spot, he will. Expect your cat to make 4 to 6 mistakes before the training is complete. So instead of getting angry or disappointed when he does, consider it an important step in the process. Look at it as one less mess to clean up on the road to a litter-free existence.

As cat owners, we tend to be a little spoiled. Until I began the training, my cats had never made a mistake. From day one they used the litter box. Unlike most dog owners, who must train the puppy to hold it in until walk time, our pets arrive virtually worry-free on that count. We're uniquely lucky in this regard, as no other domesticated animal I'm aware of buries his waste as completely and conscientiously as the cat.

Old magazines, boxes, paper: This is an easy one. In the first step of the process, you'll need to raise the box. Use old newspapers, magazines, and/or boxes to raise the litter box.

Are You Ready for This?

The main prerequisite, despite the aforementioned supplies, is an understanding of your cat. Acknowledge his likes and dislikes, and keep them in mind as you progress through the steps outlined in this book. And be creative—if any of the steps aren't working for you and your cat, examine the issue and alter the process to suit your situation.

One of my cats responded to treats and "good kitties," another was only moderately treat-motivated, and my oldest cat only responded to gentle strokes down the side of his face with his favorite brush. It's important to find something that your cat loves and to begin the process by relegating this treat or activity to the bathroom so that your cat begins to look forward to spending time there. Play games, groom, and talk with your cat in the bathroom.

If upon seeing you enter the bathroom, your cat follows, his tail upright with expectation, you know you're on the right track.

Now for the hard part. Take your personality into account. How will you react if at three a.m. your cat decides to crawl into bed with you and relieve himself? Don't laugh, it's happened. I found myself sponging down the mattress, eyes blurred, nostrils flared, and wondering if it would be possible for me to get back to sleep. But I kept my cool—that's the important part—and though the cat knew I was unhappy, he didn't feel threatened.

Always keep in mind that your cat doesn't quite understand why you want him to do this. All he really knows is that he no longer has the box he's been using for so long. He remembers how happy you were the first time he used it. And now this? So you've got to make it as painless and pleasurable as possible. Remember, you're not just encouraging him to use the toilet, you're asking him to make a fairly major lifestyle change. It's not a simple request.

Multiple Personalities

Can you train more than one cat at a time? Absolutely. You just have to be more creative, diligent, patient, and aware. The term "copycat" takes on new meaning when your star trainee begins to take on the not-so-wonderful habits of one of your other cats.

The biggest problem you're likely to have is figuring out who made the mess. Just because you caught Cat A defecating on the living room floor on Monday doesn't mean he left the deposit on the couch Tuesday. Treat your cats equally and with kindness, never assuming the cat you caught yesterday is the one who made the mistake today.

During my first experience with toilet training, I trained two cats: a one-year-old and a two-year-old. It took a lot of determination as the progress I made seemed fleeting. When training more than one cat, the steps are identical, but you have to be doubly aware of each cat's needs. Reward the correct behavior, and redirect and ignore the bad. And clean up any mistakes thoroughly, using pet odor neutralizers.

Age

It's been suggested that one wait until the kitten is six months old before beginning the process. I agree with this assessment as it's very important to make sure your kitten is well socialized and used to using the litter box. It's also important that your kitten is large enough to easily get up on the toilet and that he has the necessary dexterity to maintain his balance. Kittens are clumsy; a tiny kitten could fall in and drown. Make sure your kitten is large enough to safely use the toilet.

Just because your kitten is too small to begin the training in earnest, don't despair. Early exposure to new and varied stimulus is tantamount to creating an adaptable, secure cat. Expose your kitten to as many different places, people, and things as possible. This may result in a cat that's more adaptable and trainable and comfortable with novel situations. So begin by taking your young kitten on short car trips, taking it to friend's homes, outdoor cafés (my favorite), and to the pet store. If the kitten is old enough to leave its mother, it's old enough to explore. Capitalize on your kitten's curiosity while expanding the boundaries of its world.

Note: Make sure that your kitten has all of its shots before you expose it to places where other cats frequent: veterinarian's offices, humane organizations, and pet stores are often dangerous places for a kitten who's yet to receive its full battery of vaccinations. Make sure your kitten is in a carrier when visiting these places. And by all means, leash train him. Teaching your kitten (start as soon as he arrives) to accept a lead will enable him to enjoy the outdoors safely and in your control. While cat training is beyond the scope of this book, there are many fine books available that address this issue.

Prepare the Bathroom

For the next few months, this will be the most important room in the house. If you follow my directions, it may also become both the most enjoyable yet most worrisome room in the house. This is where your cat will change and grow—something that makes even the most secure of us anxious. Don't expect your cat to be any less so.

Begin by creating an atmosphere of warmth and fun in the bathroom. This is the room where he is to receive his special rewards. Play time. Combings. Anything your cat enjoys should be lavished on him while in the bathroom. In no time at all, he'll begin to associate the bathroom with all things wonderful.

Take EVERYTHING out of the bathroom: rugs, plants, garbage cans, even towels. You may even need to take the toilet paper off the roll. If you don't, as the process progresses, your cat may begin to go on the floor, using a towel, toilet paper, or the rug to cover the deed. Remember, cats need to cover their waste—it's one of their natural inclinations that you must work to your advantage.

If, during training, your cat decides to use the tub as his personal potty, simply leave an inch or so of water in it to dissuade him. After he begins using the toilet again (at least four or five times), you can do away with the water, but if he backslides and returns to the tub, add a little water again until he successfully transfers to the toilet.

If you have two bathrooms, all the better. One can be used for you and your family, the other, strictly for the cat during his training. If not, everyone is just going to have to be patient for the next few months. If family members grumble, just remind them that the cat is also being inconvenienced as he's encouraged to change his routine. Get the whole family to agree that this is a good thing before proceeding.

Note: Make sure you're not using one of those toilet bowl cleaners that you place in the tank and forget. As your cat becomes more and more comfortable in the bathroom, he may begin drinking out of the toilet. If he does, you want to make sure that there's nothing in there that might hurt him.

This is really important. Before you begin training your cat, you need to make sure your toilet is up to the task. Some things to consider:

- The toilet will be flushed more frequently
- Your plumbing must be able to handle flushable litter
- Other users/family members need to share the toilet
- The water level may need to be lowered

The last issue, water level, warrants a closer look. If the water level in your toilet is too high, your cat may become frightened by the splashback. If the cat gets splashed, you may have a very difficult time convincing him to use the toilet again. This brings us to The Truffle Test.

Training Tip
The Truffle Test . . . because cats don't do bidets

It's important to check your toilet's water level to ensure that your cat doesn't get splashed while doing his business. I like to take a truffle or bonbon (any flavor will do, but cherry-filled bonbons are especially expendable) and hold it about four inches above the bowl. Drop the truffle into the bowl, and watch the splash. Get the idea? If the water splashes onto the toilet seat, the water level is too high and must be adjusted before beginning the program. The first cat I trained suddenly began sitting on the toilet facing the wrong direction—so he was going on the floor rather than in the toilet. I soon realized that this only happened when it was time for a bowel movement. When I realized it was a water-level problem, getting him to return to regular use was very difficult. For months after he was completely trained, he still hesitated before a bowel movement. Don't make this mistake.

Give your cat as much time as he needs. When you realize he's gotten confused or anxious, take a step back. It may be frustrating, but don't despair, expect it and move on. It's all part of the learning process. If you get upset or anxious your cat will feel the same way. If you're calm, you'll make him feel a little more at ease. Reward him, and in time, he'll reward you.

That said, I'm going to go out on a limb and say that most cats will become completely trained in two to four months. There will be some that will require a little less time, others a little more. My oldest cat, who is as stubborn as they come, graduated in three months. My youngest, who flew through the early stages, also required nearly three months. Be patient; the rewards are just around the corner.

Now that we've got the preliminaries out of the way, it's time to begin encouraging!

The Procedure

The following steps must be completed in order, allowing your cat as much time as necessary to become comfortable with the associated task before moving on. The following pages present a high-level view of the entire process. I'll break it down further for each individual step in the coming chapters, but this gives you a good overview.

STEP 1:

Up, Up, and Away!

Procedure
- ☙ Raise the litter box until it's at the same height as the toilet.

Lessons Learned
- ☙ Despite the height of the box, it's still safe.
- ☙ The toilet is not a threat.
- ☙ Good things happen in the restroom.

STEP 2:

One Paw at a Time

Procedure

- 🐾 Put a bowl of litter in the toilet for the cat to use as his new litter box.

Lessons Learned

- 🐾 The size of the box doesn't matter.

- 🐾 Sitting with all four paws on the toilet seat keeps me dry and clean.

STEP 3:

Easy on the Sand

Procedure

- ❧ Reduce the amount of litter in the bowl until there's really not enough to cover his waste.

Lessons Learned

- ❧ I can no longer completely cover my waste.

- ❧ The human will clean the bowl after I use it.

- ❧ Sitting on the toilet seat keeps my paws dry (reinforced).

STEP 4:

Like Sands Through the Hourglass

Procedure
- ❧ Cut a dime-sized hole in the bottom of the bowl and further reduce the amount of litter.

Lessons Learned
- ❧ The litter now falls into the water.
- ❧ The bowl is still a secure, safe place.

STEP 5:

The Time They Are a-Changin'

Procedure

☙ Increase the size of the hole in the bottom of the bowl every couple of days, and continue to reduce the amount of litter.

Lessons Learned

☙ Going in the water is okay.

☙ There is less odor now.

☙ Less litter is not a bad thing.

☙ I can no longer bury my waste.

☙ There's no longer a significant ledge to brace my paws on.

STEP 6:

Building the Perfect Beast

Procedure

- ❖ Reduce the litter until there is none left.

Lessons Learned

- ❖ It's okay to go when there's no litter.

- ❖ After my waste falls in the water, it doesn't smell as bad and will be flushed away.

STEP 7:

Cat on a Cold Porcelain Throne

Procedure
- ♣ Cut away the remainder of the bottom of the bowl.

Lessons Learned
- ♣ Everything goes right through the hole.
- ♣ I can't step down and investigate anymore.

STEP 8:

Free at Last

Procedure
🐾 Remove the bowl.

Lesson Learned
🐾 I don't need no stinkin' litter!

STEP I:
Up, Up, and Away

After preparing the bathroom (see Prepare the Bathroom on page 18), place your cat's regular litter box in the bathroom beside the toilet. Let the cat get used to this setup—it shouldn't take more than a day or two. If the bathroom is where you normally locate the litter box, you're all set. Just make sure it's placed beside the toilet, or as close to the toilet as possible.

Once the cat is used to the new location, you may begin raising the box. Using newspapers, a board, or a thin, flat box, raise the litter box an inch or so off the floor. Make sure that the litter box is stable and won't slip when the cat climbs in.

If your cat is like mine, he won't have a problem with this. Leave the setup alone for a couple of days. On the third day, raise the box another inch. With the box now two inches off the floor, your cat is likely to notice that something subtle has changed. If he's fine with it, wait at least 24 hours before adding another inch. If by the time the box is three inches off the floor your cat doesn't seem to mind, try raising it two inches rather than one. If at any point your cat becomes agitated, slow down. Lower the box an inch or two and leave it there until he's comfortable again. Always proceed at his pace.

31

Continue raising the box every day or two until the box is as high as the toilet seat. It is important that you maintain a stable base for the litter box. The higher you go, the more potential for a mishap. Magazines are slippery, and as the box begins to gain some height, they become more and more unstable. Once you've got a little height, put the materials in a box to create a much more stable surface for you to build upon. You might even want to tape the litter box to the materials you're using to raise the box to make sure it doesn't slide as your cat climbs in and out. Once the litter box is at the same height as the toilet seat, your cat will likely be comfortable with the new arrangement and continue to use the box as before. Good. Your goal is to present the cat with a succession of *little* changes so you don't upset his routine. Cats, like many of us, are creatures of habit.

Remember to reward your cat. It may not seem like he's done much at this juncture, but he has. He's made a change to his routine. Reward him for his behavior each time you catch him using the elevated box and let him know how proud you are of him.

Lessons Learned

- It doesn't matter how high off the floor the litter box is, it's still a safe, clean place to do my business.
- The toilet is non-threatening.
- Good things happen to me in the bathroom—I receive rewards in the bathroom.

You know it's time to move on when . . .

- The litter box is at the same height as the toilet seat, and your cat is using the box without hesitation or fear.

Training Tip
Neatness Doesn't Count

Don't overclean the bathroom. I know, a clean bathroom not only sparkles but smells like a lemon orchard. After the training, that's okay, but for now, you don't want to use detergents and cleansers that are too fragrant or it may put your cat off the pot (many cats hate the scent of pine and citrus, for example). In the early stages, it's best to clean using fresh hot water and a minimal amount of chemical soap. Remember, your cat is very attuned to odors. Leave a little spilled litter on the top of the toilet tank, even a little on the floor (but not much, you don't want to confuse him). Clean, but don't go overboard. If you'd have no problem eating off the floor, you may be in danger of eradicating the good smells your cat needs to make the transition.

STEP 2:
One Paw at a Time

If you've completed Step 1, the litter box should now be at the same level as the toilet seat, and your cat has probably investigated the toilet on his trips to and from the box. This is great and leads us to Step 2.

Take a deep breath—it's time to do away with the litter box altogether. Empty and clean the litter box, and store it away so your cat doesn't see it. You won't be using it again, unless your cat becomes sick or too old to manage the toilet.[3]

Now, lift the toilet seat, and place the plastic mixing bowl in. The lip of the bowl should make contact with the rim of the toilet bowl, securing it in place. Lower the seat, and fill the bowl about a quarter of the way full. Use flushable litter as some will be going into the toilet.

Pick up your cat, and gently set him down on the toilet seat so that he can investigate the new setup. If he ignores it and

---

3 An elderly cat may need assistance—a carpet covered ramp will help even the most elderly of cats continue using the toilet. A sick cat should never be asked to perform this task if he is unable to or it produces undue stress.

immediately jumps down, try again. If he continues to ignore it, place his feet into the bowl so that he feels the litter there. Don't force him. Your cat has a very acute sense of smell, and even if he appears to be oblivious to it, he knows it's there.

> **Note:** If your bowl doesn't fit securely in the toilet, tape a ruler to each side of the bowl and "hang" the bowl in the toilet. Put the seat down, and the bowl will be secure. You will need to change the tape every week or two.

If all goes as planned, your cat should immediately begin using it as a litter box. If he's a small cat, he may be able to squeeze his body inside the toilet seat and use it like a traditional litter box, but in no time at all he'll realize that putting his front paws on the seat makes things more pleasant. Praise him extensively and reward him for being such a good boy.

Once they've learned that two paws on the seat is a good thing, some cats will learn to perch on the seat, with all four feet, all by themselves. Most will need some assistance. So, when you catch your cat using the bowl, simply lift one of his back paws out of the bowl, and gently place it on the seat beside his front paws. In all likelihood, he'll leave it there. Praise and reward him even if he doesn't. The next time you catch him using the bowl, place both of his back paws on the seat so all four paws are on the seat and he's in the proper position. It may take a few tries before he's comfortable with this position, but not as long as you might think. Soon he'll realize that this position keeps his feet dry, and he'll prefer it to having his feet in the bowl when he goes. Each cat is an individual though, and your cat may take longer. Generally, assisting your cat two or three times is enough to cement this new behavior in his mind. If he doesn't seem receptive to your intervention, that's okay; over time, as the procedure progresses, he will begin sitting on the toilet of his own volition.

If he makes a mistake on the floor, simply clean up the mess using your pet deodorizer, and again, show him the litter in the toilet bowl. Don't scold or get angry—it won't help. Keep your cool, and help your cat get back on track.

Lessons Learned

- The size of the box doesn't matter.
- Placing my paws on the seat keeps them from getting dirty.

You know it's time to move on when . . .

- Your cat has successfully used the new setup 4–5 times.

Training Tip
Seat Down, Lid Up!

Okay, we've all heard the joke about men forgetting to put the seat down. Well, guys, we now have a second reason to be considerate. While your cat may be able to perch directly on the ceramic bowl, it's neither as comfortable nor as stable. So remember—seat down!

But what about the lid? It's even more important that you remember to keep the lid up. Unfortunately, it's hard to remember to remind guests. I found that taping the lid up using clear box tape is effective and not very noticeable. During training, it's imperative that your cat doesn't encounter a closed lid.

STEP 3:
Easy on the Sand

Now that your cat has become accustomed to using the bowl, reduce the amount of litter. A half cup should be sufficient. It's not much, but it's important that you begin to wean him off his litter dependency. If your cat's a constant digger, this may be a difficult adjustment for him. Give him plenty of time and encouragement, and don't forget the rewards. Remember, your cat should only be receiving rewards when he performs the task at hand: urination or a bowel movement. He needs to associate good things with his litter training. If you give him rewards because he begs or just because he's cute, you'll confuse the issue and lose one of your most important tools. Resist the temptation as much as possible. As the training progresses, you'll have plenty of opportunities to reward him.

Now that there's very little litter to cover his waste, you need to clean the bowl out as soon as possible. Your cat is used to covering his waste to cut the odor. He's not going to like the fact that he can't reduce the odor as much as he has in the past. It will irritate him.

Many cats will continue to scratch around, trying to cover their waste. If you're around when he does his business, pick him up and praise him, giving him a reward to make him forget about covering his waste. Immediately clean the bowl, and set it up for its next use. If you're not home when he goes, you'll have to wait until you get home to clean the bowl. That's okay, as your cat will eventually give up on trying to cover his waste and leave the room to be rid of the odor. Some cats will wait for you to return before doing their business, so you can take care of the odor for them.

Lessons Learned

- I can no longer completely cover my waste.
- The human will clean the bowl after I use it.
- Sitting on the toilet seat keeps my paws dry.

You know it's time to move on when . . .

- Your cat has successfully used the toilet 3–4 times without feeling stressed. A stressed cat will do a lot of meowing and spend an inordinate amount of time trying to cover his waste. Reward and praise your cat, turning his stress into pleasure.

Training Tip
Constant Cleaning

While you're training your cat to use the bowl in the toilet, it's important that you clean the bowl after every use. If you're at home when he goes, stop whatever you're doing (within reason!), and clean the bowl. Until the hole is large enough for his waste to completely go through, the smell will be offensive to him (and you!). My cats tended to go in the morning, before I went to work, and within half an hour of my return, making it easy for me to clean the bowl and flush away the waste within minutes of their proud exit from the bathroom.

STEP 4:
Like Sands Through the Hourglass

At this point, your cat should be using the bowl without hesitation. If he isn't, or has recently made a mistake, give him as long as necessary to become comfortable with the new setup. If you rush him now, you may regret it.

This is a major step. Even if your cat has been a real champ up to now, he may stumble. Make sure you have a bottle of pet odor neutralizer on hand—you're likely to need it.

Okay, now it's time to make the first hole in the bottom of the bowl. Be very careful you don't hurt yourself. If you're not used to working with sharp tools, find someone to assist. Cut a very small hole in the bottom of the bowl (see the illustration) using an electric drill or a sharp cutting tool. The hole should be no larger than a dime—any larger, and I can pretty safely predict that your cat won't be having any of it!

Once you've cut the hole, replace the bowl in the toilet, and carefully pour about a half cup of litter around the hole. This should be the flushable variety as some of it will fall through the hole and into the toilet. Once your cat begins to use the new setup, his investigations will send most of the rest through.

This is a major step for your cat. He'll likely be curious as he scratches in the bowl and sees the litter slip through the hole. If you're present when this occurs and your cat seems agitated, this may be a perfect time to heap on the praise and offer a reward. This might deter him from the business at hand, but he'll soon return, more determined than before.

Maintain this setup until your cat is using the bowl with minimal stress. This is likely to take a few days, as the first couple days are likely to be rough ones.

Lessons Learned

- The litter falls into the water now.
- The bowl is still a secure, safe place to do my business.

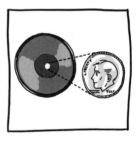

You know it's time to move on when . . .

- Your cat has successfully and comfortably used the new setup 3–4 times. This step could take up to a week to complete.

STEP 5:
The Times, They
Are a-Changin'

Increase the size of the hole in the bottom of the bowl. Slightly. Make it about the size of a nickel. A quarter is too large. Expect your cat to have as much trouble with this new hole size as he did with the first. Yep. He'll be just as anxious, so remember to heap on the praise and offer rewards. You're asking him to take another big step. Now he can see more of the water, and more litter slips through with each step.

Expect it to take a couple days for your cat to get used to the new hole size. If he's hesitant, don't move on until he's comfortable with the change. Don't rush. Relax. You'll get there, I promise.

When your cat becomes comfortable with the new hole, continue increasing the size of the hole and reducing the amount of litter used. It's important that you allow your cat plenty of time to get used to each new hole size. Do not increase the size after a single, successful use. The secret is to let the cat get used to each change before making additional changes. I suggest, as a minimal standard, three to four successful uses of the bowl before increasing the hole size and reducing the amount of litter. Remember, this is a *minimal* standard—your cat may require longer. That doesn't mean your cat is slow or less apt, just that your cat's personality dictates you slow down and breathe. So don't try to force change—work *with* him. This should not become a battle of wits but, rather, gentle suggestion.

Continue increasing the size of the hole and decreasing the amount of litter used until there's only about a one-inch ring at the bottom of the bowl and you're only using about a tablespoon of litter, sprinkled around the remaining bottom of the bowl.

As the hole gets larger, more and more of his waste slips through the hole and into the water. This is a big, confusing, alarming situation for your cat. Not only can he no longer cover most of his waste, he can't even reach it. Expect him to start a bit of phantom litter covering—scratching the toilet seat in an attempt to cover his waste, the odor, and his tracks. This is a perfect opportunity to pick him up, tell him what a good boy he is, and reward him for his brilliance.

Note: Increasing the hole size is gradual. Shoot for a 50 percent increase in size each time. If the plastic breaks, or you cut too large of a hole, don't worry. Give it a try. If your cat gets unduly anxious by the sudden change or begins regularly going outside the toilet, don't stress. Breathe. Take some of the discarded plastic from the hole you cut, and tape it back in until the size of the hole is smaller again. After your cat is again using the toilet, make the hole bigger, but not quite as big as the last time. Let him get used to this before moving on.

During this stage, you should expect your cat to get confused from time to time and make a couple of mistakes. Try not to get angry or discouraged. It's going to happen, and more than once, so chalk it up as part of the learning process. Use your pet odor neutralizer to clean up the mistake, and move on. If your cat approaches and wants to snuggle while you're cleaning, don't reciprocate. You don't want to end up rewarding inappropriate behavior. Instead, stop what you're doing, pick up the cat, and place him on the toilet. Talk to him softly about what you want him to do. He won't understand a word of it (well, I don't think so), but he will understand the tone.

Lessons Learned

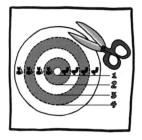

- Going in the water is okay.
- There's less odor now.
- Less litter is not a bad thing.
- I can no longer bury my waste.
- There's no longer a significant ledge to brace my paws on.

You know it's time to move on when . . .

- The bowl only has about a one-inch lip remaining on the bottom, and there is only about a tablespoon of litter. Your cat is regularly (6–8 times) using the setup with few complaints.

Training Tip
Phantom Litter

As your cat begins to use the toilet, don't be surprised if you see him scratch along the toilet seat as if he's trying to cover his waste. In most cases, this behavior will extinguish itself over time. It could take a couple weeks to a number of months before the habit is completely extinguished. It's a hard habit to break and not one you should worry about. After all, he's in the process of adopting a most wonderful new routine.

STEP 6:
Building the Perfect Beast

Now that your cat is used to going through the hole in the bottom of the bowl, it is now time to wean him off the litter completely. This may be more difficult than it sounds, as many cats are "addicted" to the smell of their litter.

For the first few days, reduce the amount of litter to about half a teaspoon or less. It's not much, and your cat may get confused. If he does, pull out the pet odor neutralizer and clean up the mess. Pick up your cat and place him on the toilet. Remember, keep your temper. I understand that it's difficult, and if you find you're having trouble, leave the house and return after a nice walk. Then, upon your return, take your cat to the toilet, and gently place him on the seat. He'll probably jump right off, without investigation. That's okay. Pick him up again, and place him there again. Praise him warmly, and wait for the next go round.

Once your cat is used to this new situation and has successfully used the toilet three to four times, clean the bowl, and don't put any litter in the bowl. If the cat refuses to use the bowl, you may have to go back to sprinkling about a half teaspoon of litter in the bowl to get him to use it again. If he still balks at the litter-free bowl, see A Note on Changes on page 63.

Lessons Learned

- It's okay to go to the bathroom when there is no litter.
- After my waste falls in the water, it doesn't smell as bad.

You know it's time to move on when . . .

- Your cat uses the bowl with less than a tablespoon of litter 3–4 times.

Training Tip
Cruel to Be Kind

If at any stage of the process your cat decides that taking a dump on the couch is a more desirable activity, he may be having a negative response to change. Slow down, and back up a step if necessary. If you didn't heed my warning about "slowly" increasing the size of the hole, you may have asked for too much at once. Buy another bowl if necessary, and put a much smaller hole in it. If your cat still decides he wants none of it, lock him in the bathroom overnight. Provide him with food and water, but take out any towels, garbage cans, rugs, etc., and partially fill the tub with water so he doesn't decide the tub is a more adequate substitution for the box.

If, the next morning, he still hasn't used the facilities, refresh his food and water, and leave him in the bathroom until he does. Though this may sound cruel, it isn't. Your cat is refusing to use the

bowl not because he doesn't like using it but because it no longer makes sense to him. Once you get him using it again, despite his apprehensions, he'll soon realize that, though things are now different, using the toilet is a suitable alternative to the old way of doing things.

STEP 7:
Cat on a Cold Porcelain Throne

Okay, now that you've got your cat to use the bowl without any litter, you're just about there. Cut away the final inch from the bottom of the bowl, making it completely bottomless. Your cat is a constant investigator, and he's sure to notice the missing ledge right away. And again, he may be put off from using it. Don't despair. If he has an accident, clean up the mess, then gently pick up your cat, and place him on the toilet seat. By now, he knows exactly what that means.

If you're training a young cat or kitten, he will likely need to go to the bathroom within 10–20 minutes of eating a meal. As soon as you see any exploratory behavior, you can encourage him to use the toilet. If you see him enter the bathroom and explore the toilet, encourage and reward him. If he jumps up and then down multiple times, confused at the new setup, simply pick him up, and place him on the toilet, talking to him in a soft and encouraging tone. Repeat this as many times as necessary until he uses the toilet.

Note: If possible, make this change on a weekend, when you'll be home to watch and assist your cat through this near-final stage.

Lessons Learned

- Everything goes right through the hole and into the water.

You know it's time to move on when . . .

- Your cat has successfully used the toilet 3–4 times.

Training Tip
The Double Moxie

Cats have a very acute sense of smell which they use to make decisions before they act. Many cats will even stop eating when they have extreme nasal passage blockage, so it should come as no surprise that when you take away the last trace of litter, the bathroom no longer smells like a place to do his business.

That's where the double moxie comes in. To aid your cat in the transition, apply double-stick tape to the underside of the toilet seat and press granules of litter to it. Clean up any spillage, then lower the toilet seat. The cat should not be

able to see the litter, but he will be able to smell it. This is a temporary measure that won't be necessary in most cases, but if your cat loses interest in the toilet once the last traces of litter are gone, this technique may help you reorient him.

STEP 8:
Free at Last

Okay, this is it, the final change you're going to request of your cat. It's another major request, so don't take it too lightly. It's time to remove the plastic bowl.

When you remove the bowl, your cat may or may not take exception. Some cats persist in running their forepaws over the bowl before going, so removal of the bowl will be very major indeed. Other cats, now used to the smell of the water, will barely notice. Again, this is not an indicator of your cat's intelligence but rather a manifestation of his personality. Give him what he needs. If he begins to go in inappropriate places, replace the bowl for a couple more days and then try again. It may be necessary to lock him in the bathroom overnight so that he'll see no better option than to use the facilities. Once he's used them, he's likely to realize it wasn't all that bad, and you'll have done it! A completely toilet-trained cat!

One last note: Just because you've completed the training and have given a big sigh of relief, your cat's not aware of this. He may be anxious, expecting the next big change. For the next couple of weeks, watch him carefully. Continue to praise him for a job well done but not as effusively as you did before. It's now time to wean him off the rewards as well. Slowly but surely, wean him from the constant praise and rewards over the next few weeks. It's important that he doesn't become dependent on the rewards and discontinue his new behavior after they have stopped.

An occasional reward and praise are still in order. After all, we're talking about an incredible feat, one that no other household pet is capable of. He's a special creature and deserves to be reminded, so remember to indulge him every once in a while.

Lessons Learned

- I can do this.
- You know, the litter box was nice, but this is just as good.
- I don't need no stinkin' litter box!

You know you're done when . . .

- You realize you've bought your last jug of litter, scooped your last clump, and you're grinning so broad it's beginning to hurt.

Training Tip
Crying for Attention

At some point, your cat may become stressed and decide that this is no longer fun. If he goes into the bathroom and begins crying and wandering around, watch him, but don't console him. If you do, you might encourage a bad habit. If he begins to go in an inappropriate spot, pick him up mid-stream, and place him on the toilet. Once he's started, he won't stop. You may have a urine trail to clean up, but it'll be worth it; he'll make the connection again. Reward him after he does his business. He's just made a big step and needs to be reminded of it. Now I'd love to tell you that you'll only have to do this once, but it may take two to three times to set the behavior solidly in his mind again. Your cat is simply confused by the process, the lack of odor, and the loss of routine. He needs to firmly establish a new routine. This is nothing to worry about. Keep your cool, redirect his behavior, and watch him get over his confusion and begin regularly using the toilet.

So What Do You Do When He Just Won't Use the Toilet?

If, during any phase of the training, your cat stops using the toilet, it's probably due to one of the following reasons:

- You're moving too fast
- A recent change has confused the cat
- He no longer can smell the litter and has become confused

If you're moving too quickly, slow down. Back up to a stage your cat is comfortable with, and begin again from there. In some cases, you may need to buy a new bowl or reduce the hole's size using duct tape and the cutaway pieces. Do it. On the other hand, what if, after patiently guiding him through the steps and completing the training, he suddenly decides he doesn't want to use the toilet? Don't worry, this is not as bad as it appears. Often, when all traces of litter are gone, your cat will get confused. The lack of familiar odors may be perplexing to him. I had this problem with two of the cats I trained, and although stressful, the solution is basically simple.

You'll need a couple of days—a weekend will do—to reorient your cat to the toilet. If the problems begin midweek, confine your cat to the bathroom when you're away. Take out everything he could use to cover his waste—toilet paper, towels, even the garbage can. Make sure there's plenty of food and water and a couple of his favorite toys. Put a couple inches of water in the tub. No cat beds. Unfortunately, a bed may seem like a suitable spot to do his business when he's in this state. In the small, empty space of the bathroom, your cat will more than likely decide that the toilet is the only suitable place to go.

When the weekend arrives, you'll be able to watch him. When you see him pawing around, looking for a place to go, take him to the bathroom and place him on the toilet. He may immediately use it or jump off and look for a "better" spot. Every time he begins the pawing, pick him up and place him on the toilet again. After four or five of these trips, he's likely to use the toilet. If he doesn't, close the bathroom door and leave him there until he does. Reward him for his good behavior, and within a couple of days, he should be choosing the toilet on his own again.

A Note on Changes

I've made the mistake, on more than one occasion, of making a change to the setup (enlarging the hole, removing the litter, etc.) on days when I wouldn't be home until very late. This is not a good idea. Your cat needs you to reassure him on those days and to reward him for his intelligence and flexibility when he gets it right. Don't forget the rewards—especially in the early days. If you have a night out planned, a late meeting, or won't be coming home after work, make that a "business-as-usual day" and hold off on the big changes for days when you'll be present to support him in his endeavors.

A Note About Failure

The reason why many people fail is that they don't give the cat enough time to accept one change before asking for another. And they give up rather than regroup. The training is messy and a lot of work. We all would like to see an end to it, and besides, we've got an especially smart cat, right? Right and wrong. Your cat's intelligence has no bearing on how long it will take for him to accept the toilet bowl. In fact, a clever cat may not see a reason for the changes requested and require more time and patience to accept even the smallest deviation.

Cutting a tiny hole in the bottom of the plastic bowl may not seem like a big request to you, but it is to your cat. So if you enlarge the hole the very next day, before he's gotten over the last change, you're asking for a revolt. By the time the training is done, your cat will have accepted numerous changes that he didn't request, want, or need. The way he sees it, the litter box thing was going well. Why fix it? So keep this in mind, and be patient. If you do, your cat will reward you by adopting a clean, healthy, new habit.

On a related note, if you have a business trip or a vacation planned within the next four months, it's not a good time to begin the training. Even if you have someone as dedicated as you are willing to continue the training in your absence, it's not a good idea. Your cat needs consistency, and any disruption in his routine may lead to confusion and a refusal of the whole process.

Don't Stop Now

Once you've trained your cat to use the toilet, you won't want to stop there. Contrary to popular belief, cats *can* be trained. There's a lot we don't understand about our cats—their mode of communication is both simplistic and complicated at the same time. Simplistic in what researchers have been able to discern, complex in the many mysterious ways that have yet to be understood.

My oldest cat, Grey, seemed very standoffish at times. When I was training him to use the toilet, he'd run from me when I tried to pick him up and tell him how wonderful he was. So I thought, this isn't really working. I'm bugging him rather than encouraging him. Then something amazing happened. Grey started waiting until I got home to do his business. It didn't matter if I was early or late, he'd go into the bathroom and do his business within 15 minutes of my arrival. Even on days when I was really late.

Part of being a cat owner is entering the world of a wild animal. It's been said that the level of domestication of the house cat is questionable, with some authors going so far as to suggest that they may not be domesticated at all.

Read as much literature as you can on cats, but don't take any of it as gospel. Continue to question, and make observations for yourself as you share your life with your cat. Most of what I've shared here is based on firsthand experiences. The things I "know" about cats are based on observation and are no more valid than the observations you—or anyone else—have made on the subject.

A Note on Furniture

Okay, here's the bad news. Your cat may urinate on your bed or other pieces of furniture. If he does, mop up as much of it as you can, then follow the instructions on your bottle of pet odor neutralizer. This is the most difficult issue you will have to deal with, and when it happens, no blather about greener pastures will make it any easier. I know. I've been there. But the odor does come out. It may take multiple applications and a bit of patience, but the neutralizers should do the job.

Why do they choose furniture so frequently? I have my suspicions, but I don't really know for sure. What I do believe is that it's not a retaliatory act. No matter how much it appears so, remember, it's part of the mystery of cathood.

Do No Harm

This should go without saying, but cats are not dogs. Yes, they're trainable. Yes, they learn their names and can learn to come when called. And yes, they consider themselves part of the family. But there are even more ways in which they differ.

There is a common belief that cats are more independent because they haven't been domesticated as long as dogs have. That may be true, but it may have nothing to do with their behaviors and how dependent or independent they are.

That said, whenever someone points at a cat and declares its nature, I bristle. While there are similarities among members of a breed and among cats in general, there are no absolutes. This may be due in part to the fact that they haven't been as selectively bred as dogs. Despite the popularity of hybrid crosses, there really aren't many extremes in body size and temperament among cats. Cats have personalities, and cats—even littermates—can vary wildly in their temperament, amount of independence, and ability to cope with novel situations.

Cats just *are*.

But there is one thing that seems to be a universal, and that is their inability to understand the concept of punishment. Positive reinforcement, in the form of a treat or some special attention, works wonders, but never, ever physically or mentally punish a cat. Even squirt bottles are off-limits because, as soon as your cat associates the squirted water with you, you've damaged the trust bond. That damage is not easy to repair either. Unlike dogs, a Scooby Snack won't do. The cat may not even let you get close enough to give him the snack if he feels your behavior is unpredictable and dangerous.

Look at it this way: cats don't understand the concept of "no." When you tell your cat what to do, he often will look at you as if you're crazy. It just doesn't compute. They are not pack animals. They do not look to a leader for confirmation and worth. They are independent souls that have decided to share their lives with you because you are good to them, you share your food, you provide them shelter, and you give them love. They'll give it back if you behave and prove worthy of their trust.

So remember, when your cat makes a mistake, don't rub his nose in it, shout at him, or swat him with a rolled-up newspaper. It won't work, and the harm it could do to your relationship may be lasting. Treat your cat like a roommate: coerce better behavior, but never punish.

Do no harm. Change the parameters so the bad behavior is no longer possible and a better option has been presented—and you'll find success in virtually anything you set out to teach your cat, including using the toilet.

101 Uses for Your Litter Box (Now That You're Done)

Now that your cats are no longer tied to the litter box, what should you do with it? Well, don't throw it away just yet! You may be able to find a use for it after all. Here are a hundred and one suggestions to get you started—including ten to color!

Note: While most of the following suggestions are simple and require few or no tools, some may require some specialized knowledge. That said, there's a DIY project in this list for everyone.

1. Toss crumpled paper balls into it for your cat to retrieve for a fun **cat game**

2. Add some stones, an inch or so of water, and a palm tree—instant **turtle habitat**

3. Throw some dirt and wheatgrass seed in the box for a large **cat grass planter**

4. Elevate your view by using the box as a **computer monitor stand**

5. Use it as a **toy box** for all those catnip mice and sponge balls

6. Fill it with water, floating toys, and feeder fish for a **wild time** for all

7. Store all those bits and bobs in your new **junk box**

8. Use it as a **recycle bin,** and recycle all those empty cat tins

9. Your guests will sit up and take notice of the ultimate **soup tureen**

10. A gelatin mold for the next family get-together

11. Paint it, and make an extra-large **shadow box** for your Chia Pet collection

12. If it's a high-walled model, cut a cat-sized hole in the bottom and the side, turn it upside down, and make a **cat playhouse** out of it

13. Store all those pens and paints in a repurposed **art supply box**

14. If you've got a green thumb, create a practical **weeding box**

15. Create a **worm farm,** and raise your own bait

16. **Donate** it to a cat shelter or a less fortunate friend who's still using litter

17. Cover it with plastic wrap to make a **seedling greenhouse**

18. Add a couple of handles, and create a handy **tool box**

19. Strap a dog to one end, and make a **dogsled** for your cat

20. Create an unsinkable boat for cats and other small animals

21. Add a handle, and use it as a **replacement bureau drawer**

22. Upend it, and use it as an **under-desk footrest**

23. Use it as a **brick-making mold,** and finally take care of that catio project you've been planning

24. Use it as a **temporary tank** when cleaning out the aquarium

25. Got a couple boxes? Add rope handles, and make **stilts** for your kids

26. Fill it with water and lily pads, and then add fish for a **koi pond**

27. Fill it with shoes or sweaters, and use it as an **under-bed storage box**

28. When cooking for the whole crew, use it as an **extra large mixing bowl**

29. Start a shoe shining business and use it as a **shoe shining stand**

30. Relive the past with your very own medieval catapult

31. Create a **baby bird care station** when little birdies drop by

32. Spitting may be a dirty habit, but a **spittoon** shows you have class

33. A **baby tub** for the little ones

34. An ecologically responsible **compost bin**

35. A **feral cat trap** for the neighborhood catch-and-release program

36. A **mail slot mailbox catcher** to keep things tidy

37. A **diaper pail** for the nappies (covered boxes only, please)

38. A **step stool** to help you put the cats' favorite toys out of reach

39. A **punch bowl** for your next party

40. An airplane for cats that like heights (advanced users only)

41. A **pill box** for those with a lot of meds

42. A **dirty dish bin** for your favorite restaurant

43. A **kitten corral** to keep the little dickens from destroying your home while you sleep

44. A **terrarium** for your hermit crab collection

45. A **raffle ticket box** for the church social

46. A **paint roller tray** for your next home improvement job

47. An automobile **oil change bucket**

48. Using anything but catgut, string it up for a **custom stringed instrument**

49. Got a pair of boxes? Make a pair of awesome **snowshoes**

50. Add water and Epsom salts for a relaxing foot soaker

51. A **magazine storage box** for those cat magazines you can't part with

52. A **bed table** for serving breakfast in bed

53. A **small dog pannier**

54. A **basket** for your vegetable garden harvest

55. A **bicycle cargo basket** for those quick trips to the store

56. A **mop bucket**

57. An **earthquake preparedness kit** for all your disaster supplies

58. Fill it with festive goodies, and create a **gift basket** for someone you love

59. When busking on the weekend, use it as a **tip box**

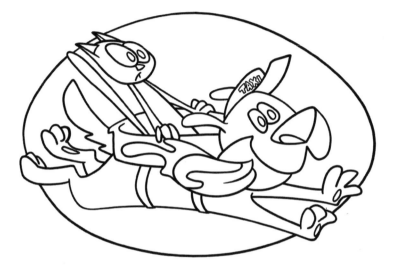

60. A dog-powered taxicab (or Uber vehicle, if that's your bent)

61. Add a cord and wheels to make a **child's wagon or pull toy**

62. Create sand blocks using it as a **massive sand castle construction assistance device (MSCCAD)**

63. Fill them with classics to create a **portable bookshelf**

64. Placed by the fireplace, it works as a perfect **tinderbox**

65. Use it as a **bread box** for your freshly baked loaves

66. Use it as a **firewood box** for those pressed wood logs

67. Turn it upside down, and use it as a **drum** in your garage band

68. Add a couple of dividers, and you've got one nifty **wine rack**

69. You can create a **rake and broom holder** by cutting holes in the short ends to thread your tools and secure them in place against a wall

70. Add a pillow, and create a pet bed for the discerning cat

71. Before you throw out the bathwater, create a **baby bathtub**

72. Add a crockery pitcher, and you have a **wash basin**

73. Donate to a school in need for use as a **cubby drawer** for storing art supplies, etc.

74. A **window planter box** for your catnip plants

75. A **Salvation Army Santa donation bucket** would ring in the new year right

76. A **dirty clothes basket** for laundry day duties

77. A **church donation plate** that's sure to encourage large donations

78. A **shoe box** for your Sunday best

79. A **picnic basket** with enough room for a feast for the entire family

80. A race car—just add wheels and engine

81. A **pet coffin** for that inevitable heart-wrenching day

82. An **ice bucket** for your wet bar

83. A **baptismal font** for animal baptisms

84. A **DIY speaker case** for the audiophiles among us

85. A **mushroom cultivation environment** for an endless supply of fun(gus)

86. Paint it up, and create a classy **lamp shade**

87. Anchor it to a tree stump or pedestal to create a **birdbath**

88. Add a lid and padlock for a totally secure **ballot box**

89. Put the box on your head, secure it with a strip of lace tied under your chin, and you'll be the talk of the garden party in your stunningly unique **sun hat**

90. A sandbox for the kids

91. A **faux bullet-proof vest** for the wannabe fashionistas

92. A **Christmas ornament box** to store your most treasured decorations

93. An **Easter basket** the bunny can't resist filling

94. A **mini basketball hoop** for game day

95. A **miniature golf tunnel** for your backyard course

96. A **toy train tunnel and overpass** for those who dream of electric trains

97. A **string telephone resonance box** for the Alexander Graham Bell in all of us

98. A custom computer game enthusiast **gaming rig case**

99. A **gold pan** (just add holes)

100. A **record album crate** for your trendy vinyl collection

101. A hot-air balloon basket to rise above it all

Further Reading

Books that are little more than a list of breed descriptions and basic grooming concerns are a dime a dozen. Once you've bought one, you won't need another. The following list represents some of my favorite cat books—books that focus on understanding your cat and creating a caring environment. Many are old and out of print, but all of them are fascinating.

Cat Daddy: What the World's Most Incorrigible Cat Taught Me About Life, Love, and Coming Clean

Jackson Galaxy

Tarcher, 2014

Host of *My Cat From Hell* tells his story of how his love and respect for cats helped him find the same for himself.

Cat Sense: How the New Feline Science Can Make You a Better Friend to Your Pet

John Bradshaw

Basic Books, 2014

Interesting fact-filled book that examines the theories behind the development of the modern-day cat as it relates to cat behavior.

Cat Watching

Desmond Morris

Crown Publishers, Inc., 1986

This is another oldie but a goodie. You'll have to buy this on the used market or check it out of the library, but it's worth reading. This is more of an FAQ than a traditional cat book as Morris fashioned the book as a series of questions and answers on cat behavior. The author wrote a follow-up, *Cat Lore* (Crown Publishers, Inc., 1988) that provides even more answers.

Cat World: A Feline Encyclopedia

Desmond Morris

Penguin Reference, 1997

An incredible volume. More information about cats than most books on the market. Highly entertaining. For answers to common behavioral questions, check out *Cat Watching* and *Cat Lore* by the same author. It doesn't get much better than this.

Catify to Satisfy

Jackson Galaxy and Kate Benjamin

Tarcher Perigee, 2015

Jackson Galaxy, host of *My Cat from Hell*, and Kate Benjamin provide a number of home projects that will help you rethink your home design with your cat in mind. The book is chock-full of full-color photographs of home projects designed to improve the lives of your feline friends.

Good Owners, Great Cats

Brian Kilcommons and Sarah Wilson

Warner Books, 1995

Great book with a focus on cat behavior and training issues.

The Lion in the Living Room: How House Cats Tamed Us and Took Over the World
Abigail Tucker
Simon & Schuster, 2016

With a title like that, it's gotta be good. Abigail Tucker, a science and nature writer, takes on the topic of how the housecat came to hold such an important role in our lives. Along the way, she provides dozens of facts, quirks, and reasons for our fascination with this marvelous animal.

Supercat: Raising the Perfect Feline Companion
Dr. Michael W. Fox
Howell Book House, 1990

The single most important volume for the new kitten owner. This book is important in that it concerns itself with early socialization and the importance of creating a stimulating environment for your cat. All prospective cat owners should read this before bringing the new kitten home.

The Trainable Cat: A Practical Guide to Making Life Happier for You and Your Cat
John Bradshaw
Basic Books, 2016

Bradshaw provides a good argument for training your cats and explains what you need to know to train your cats to come when called, accept medication, and a myriad of other things that many cat owners feel their cats are incapable of. He provides all this in clear, concise prose that's sure to enhance your cat's life and strengthen the human/cat bond.

Understanding Cats: Their History, Nature, and Behavior
Roger Tabor
A Reader's Digest Book, 1995
The name says it all. A very good book, filled with great photographs. I can also recommend *Understanding Your Cat* (St. Martin's Press, 1974) by the same author.

Collaborators

GreyGrey

GreyGrey and his younger brother were the first two cats I ever trained. GreyGrey was a very sweet cat and liked his treats just fine, but his two favorite things in the world were getting the side of his face brushed with a rubber-pronged brush and iceberg lettuce. Those two special treats were doled out primarily as rewards during the training. Despite his sweet disposition, he was also stubborn as the day is long. I had my doubts at first, but he ended up taking to it and setting the groundwork for this book.

Raccoon

Raccoon was a shy guy: the kind of cat who likes being in your presence but isn't into all that touchy-feely stuff. Definitely the strong, silent type. He did like to fetch though, and he never turned down a good treat. I taught Raccoon and GreyGrey simultaneously, and when things got serious, it was the first and only time that Raccoon meowed his concerns. Hearing his voice as he questioned what was going on was worrisome—would he make the transition? He did. With flying colors.

Cougar

Cougar was the fastest study. Relatively so. He just whizzed through the initial steps, and I was so proud of him! That he was smart was obvious, but at times, I felt like he was training me rather than the other way around. He seemed to be saying, "Hurry up, I got this!" every step of the way. He was an F1 Chausie; his mother was a Bengal and his father a 30-pound jungle cat. Oh, did I mention he was smart? Anyway, a month or so into the training and he was almost done. Everything I threw at him, he accepted with aplomb. Until he didn't, and started going everywhere but the toilet. I ramped the program back and virtually started over. Cougar took to it again, and the slower (but not slow) process worked like a charm. He became an outstanding toileteer.

Fenix

A year after I got Cougar, I got Fenix, another F1 Chausie. He and Cougar had the same jungle cat father, but Fenix's mother was an Abyssinian. They looked very different, but both were smart, headstrong animals. Because Fenix was a "little" kitten when he arrived, I brought out the litter box until he was old enough to be trained. Despite the fact that Cougar was already trained, he used the box during this time, often going in after the kitten and covering his waste for him. So when the kitten was about five months old, I put away the box and began anew. Even though Cougar was well aware of what was going on, he approached it as if it were his first time. Three months later, they were both well trained.

Eleanor

Eleanor, a Bengal, is the smallest cat I've ever had. She may have been the runt of the litter as she was the last one left (and she's a beauty, so her siblings must have been spectacular). Teaching her, at around six months, was pretty easy. She was still in that mode of following her big brother around, so if it was okay with him, it was okay with her. As I write this, Eleanor is about three years old and just entering the cuddly phase.

Puma

Puma, an F2 Chausie, was trained at six months of age. At the same time, he went through leash training and a transition to a raw diet. At the time, I didn't realize this was a lot to ask. Because he was going through so much, he took longer than the other cats to train. But I gave him the time he needed, and he learned like the rest of them. He's a big, beautiful kitten with a sweet, playful disposition. The main reason he took longer was because he was going to the bathroom outside, on our walks. Because of this, he didn't go on the toilet as often, meaning I had to leave the setups in place longer to give him the opportunity to get used to the changes. Because of this, I experienced more accidents than is normal. In fact, he probably made more mistakes than all the other cats I trained combined. Fortunately, those mistakes were pretty much relegated to the bathroom, so cleanup was quick and painless. So if you're training an inside/outside cat, you might want to make him an inside-only cat during the training period, or accept the fact that the training may take longer.

About the Creators

Clifford Brooks

Clifford works and writes in the San Francisco Bay Area. In addition to cat books, his fiction has been published in a number of small press and professional publications. During the day, he manages a technical writing team for a major publisher of security software. His evenings are spent attending to his obsessions: his two cats, Eleanor and Puma; his carnivorous plant collection; random acts of art; and hanging out in coffee shops where the sound of the frother serves as his personal muse.

Stephanie Medeiros

When asked to draw an assortment of goofy cats with toilets, illustrator Stephanie Medeiros couldn't resist. A friend of the author and longtime keeper of her own two goofy cats, building the visual content for the book was a fun, creative process of both observation and collaboration. With a strong foundation in traditional art, Stephanie attained her degree in animation from the Academy of Art University in San Francisco. She now resides in Colorado, growing a career as an independent graphic artist. Her strength and inspiration comes from her partner, her cats, and the wilderness that surrounds her.

Progress Journal

Step 1: Up, Up, and Away

Start date:_____

_____
_____
_____
_____
_____
_____
_____
_____
_____
_____
_____
_____
_____
_____

It's time to move on when:
The litter box is at the same height as the toilet seat, and your cat is using the box without hesitation or fear.

Completion date:_____

Step 2: One Paw at a Time

Start date:_____

_____
_____
_____
_____
_____
_____
_____
_____
_____
_____
_____
_____
_____
_____

It's time to move on when:
Your cat has successfully used the new setup 4–5 times.

Completion date:_____

Step 3: Easy on the Sand

Start date:_____

It's time to move on when:
Your cat has successfully used the toilet 3–4 times without feeling stressed. A stressed cat will do a lot of meowing and spend an inordinate amount of time trying to cover his waste. Reward and praise your cat, turning his stress into pleasure.

Completion date:_____

Step 4: Like Sands Through the Hourglass

Start date:_____

_____
_____
_____
_____
_____
_____
_____
_____
_____
_____
_____
_____
_____

It's time to move on when:
Your cat has successfully and comfortably used the new setup 3–4 times.

Completion date:_____

Step 5: The Times, They Are a-Changin'

Start date:_____

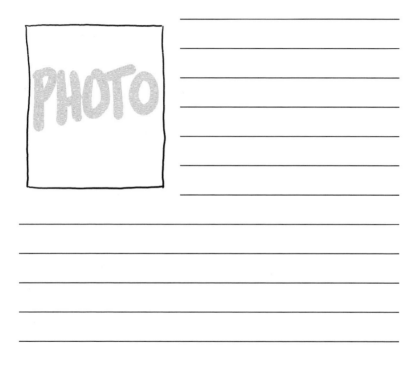

It's time to move on when:

The bowl only has about a one-inch lip remaining on the bottom, and there is only about a tablespoon of litter. Your cat is regularly (6–8 times) using the setup with few complaints.

Completion date:_____

Step 6: Building the Perfect Beast

Start date:_____

It's time to move on when:
Your cat uses the bowl with less than a tablespoon of litter 3–4 times.

Completion date:_____

Step 7: Cat on a Cold Porcelain Throne

Start date:_____

PHOTO

_____

_____

_____

_____

_____

_____

_____

_____

_____

_____

_____

_____

_____

_____It's time to move on when:
Your cat has successfully used the toilet 3–4 times.

Completion date:_____

Step 8: Free at Last

Start date:_____

_____
_____
_____
_____
_____
_____
_____
_____

_____
_____
_____
_____
_____
_____

You know you're done when:
You realize you've bought your last jug of litter, scooped your last clump, and you're grinning so broad it's beginning to hurt.

Completion date:_____

Show Your Pride!

You can purchase some of Stephanie Medeiros's hilarious designs on T-shirts, mugs, and other items. Let the world know that you share your pad with a toilet-trained cat!

DARLINGS, I GAVE UP LITTER AGES AGO

We're not saying that toilet-trained cats are better than their litter-addicted brethren, but they might be.

INNER PEACE

Look up "nirvana" on Catapedia, and you're sure to find the path to litter independence.

For information on outfitting your body and soul, visit the author's site today: www.cliffordbrooks.com

Check out these other books about cats from Skyhorse Publishing!

Cooking for Two: Your Cat & You
Delicious Recipes for You and Your Favorite Feline
by Brandon Schultz & Lucy Schultz-Osenlund

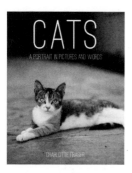

CATS
A Portrait in Pictures and Words
by Charlotte Fraser

Test Your Cat's IQ Genius Edition
Confirm Your Cat's Undiscovered Genius!
by Simon Holland